T0001911

GLENN HASCALL

READ IT!

PRAY IT!

WRITE IT!

DRAW IT!

A
FAITH-BUILDING
ACTIVITY BOOK
FOR
PRE-TEEN BOYS

DO IT!

BARBOUR **kidz**
A Division of Barbour Publishing

© 2024 by Barbour Publishing, Inc.

Print ISBN 978-1-63609-790-9

All rights reserved. No part of this publication may be reproduced or transmitted for commercial purposes, except for brief quotations in printed reviews, without written permission of the publisher. Reproduced text may not be used on the World Wide Web.

Churches and other noncommercial interests may reproduce portions of this book without the express written permission of Barbour Publishing, provided that the text does not exceed 500 words or 5 percent of the entire book, whichever is less, and that the text is not material quoted from another publisher. When reproducing text from this book, include the following credit line: "From *Read It! Pray It! Write It! Draw It! Do It!: A Faith-Building Activity Book for Pre-Teen Boys*, published by Barbour Publishing, Inc. Used by permission."

Scripture quotations are taken from the New Life Version copyright © 1969 and 2003 by Barbour Publishing, Inc., Uhrichsville, Ohio, 44683. All rights reserved.

Published by Barbour Publishing, Inc., 1810 Barbour Drive, Uhrichsville, Ohio 44683, www.barbourbooks.com

Our mission is to inspire the world with the life-changing message of the Bible.

Member of the
Evangelical Christian
Publishers Association

Printed in China.

001898 0224 HA

CONTENTS

KNOWING WHO GOD CREATED YOU TO BE

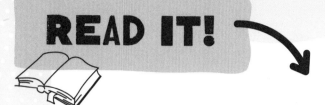

READ IT!

Christ made everything in the heavens and on the earth. He made everything that is seen and things that are not seen. He made all the powers of heaven. Everything was made by Him and for Him.
COLOSSIANS 1:16

God could create anything He wanted. And He chose to make *you*! He also made the stars, the universe, the planets, and so much more—all for your enjoyment. But why did He choose to make you? While God certainly doesn't need to be friends with the planets, He *does* want to be close to you. Jesus said in John 15:15, "I do not call you servants. . . . I call you friends."

You don't need to be perfect to be God's friend. Nope! Just as you are, He invites you to accept the greatest invitation you'll ever receive. And He leaves it up to you to decide: Will you follow God, or will you say no to being His close friend?

It's easy to think I was made to be a gamer or play sports, God. And I have lots of friends. But have I been *Your* friend? Help me to understand how important it is to choose You, to learn from You, and to accept Your great invitation for my life.

....

....

....

....

....

....

....

....

....

....

....

....

....

....

WRITE IT!

Make a list of things you can do to show
you've said yes to being friends with God.

....

....

....

....

....

....

....

....

....

....

....

....

....

....

....

Draw a picture that shows how God's friendship has made your life better.

DRAW IT!

DO IT!

Think about all the things that impress you about God's creation. Talk to a friend or family member about God and everything He made. Remember that God made this world beautiful, but He's always loved you more. It's okay to tell God thanks. He'd love to hear from you right now!

What did you learn from Colossians 1:16 and John 15:15?

....

....

....

....

....

....

....

....

....

....

....

....

....

KNOWING GOD'S WORD

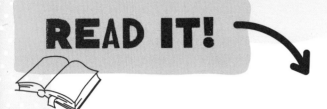

READ IT!

All the Holy Writings are God-given and are made alive by Him. Man is helped when he is taught God's Word. It shows what is wrong. It changes the way of a man's life. It shows him how to be right with God. It gives the man who belongs to God everything he needs to work well for Him.
2 TIMOTHY 3:16–17

God included very important things in His Word, the Bible—and He said you should learn from what was written in its pages. The words of the Bible can clear up confusing issues and guide you in the right direction when you have a tough choice to make. Psalm 119:105 says this about God's Word: "Your Word is a lamp to my feet and a light to my path."

The Bible is more than a big, impressive book that looks good sitting on a shelf; it brings wisdom to things you don't understand, and it helps you to know the very best way to go—God's way!

Your Word makes truth come to life, Lord. Stop me from thinking of Your Word as something I must obey for fear of being punished. Help me to remember that the words of the Bible are the words of a friend who only wants the very best for me.

WRITE IT!

What are some qualities of God that make Him the very best friend you'll ever have? Make a list below.

....

....

....

....

....

....

....

....

....

....

....

....

....

....

....

....

Draw a picture that shows God's Word being a light to your path.

DRAW IT!

DO IT!

Think of one thing you know God wants you to do, and then do it. Then think of another—do it too! Spend time reading the Bible and discovering what other things God wants you to do for Him. Share what you're learning with a friend. Ask your friend if he'd like to join you on your journey of obeying God's Word.

What did you learn from 2 Timothy 3:16–17 and Psalm 119:105?

BEING CAREFUL WITH YOUR THOUGHTS

READ IT!

Christian brothers, keep your minds thinking about whatever is true, whatever is respected, whatever is right, whatever is pure, whatever can be loved, and whatever is well thought of. If there is anything good and worth giving thanks for, think about these things.
PHILIPPIANS 4:8

You start your day thinking about God, and then somewhere along the way you get distracted. Somehow you quit paying attention to God and begin thinking about something else. Sometimes you're even ashamed of what crept into your mind. You might even be mad at yourself for thinking something you *really* didn't want to think about. Colossians 3:2 reminds us, "Keep your minds thinking about things in heaven."

When you really want to obey and do what God's Word says, then you should ask God for His help. Then read Philippians 4:8 again—this is a great way to learn the kinds of things that can help you be careful with your thoughts.

I want to be careful with my thoughts, Father God. I want to have thoughts that focus on You. I want to remember things that are true, right, and good. And I want to be thankful for all those things! I want to show You my love by being careful about the things I think about.

Make a list of things you have thought about today. Reread the list of good things to think about from Philippians 4:8, and then place a check mark by the thoughts in your list that you think would be pleasing to God.

....

....

....

....

....

....

....

....

....

....

....

....

....

Draw a picture of one of your good thoughts. Reread Philippians 4:8 to help you get started.

DRAW IT!

DO IT!

You get to decide how much time you spend thinking about something. You get to choose what's worth thinking about. How do your thoughts affect your actions? Make a list of all the good things you can think about today. Do your very best to focus on those things. Ask God to help you so your mind doesn't get distracted.

What did you learn from Philippians 4:8 and Colossians 3:2?

BEING SURE OF WHAT YOU CAN'T SEE (FAITH!)

Faith is being sure we will get what we hope for. It is being sure of what we cannot see. God was pleased with the men who had faith who lived long ago. Through faith we understand that the world was made by the Word of God. Things we see were made from what could not be seen.

HEBREWS 11:1–3

Big things happen when God speaks. He creates with His words! The entire world and universe came into being when God spoke. Isn't that amazing?

God created language so He could communicate with you. Believing that His words are true and important is a big part of faith. Second Corinthians 5:7 says, "Our life is lived by faith. We do not live by what we see in front of us."

God does what you can't do—things that seem impossible!—and He does it all *for* you. He loves. He forgives. And He provides things you can't earn or buy. When you say yes to a friendship with God, you may not see everything He does, but faith helps you believe the things you can't see! Faith helps you understand that God is big, wise, amazing, loving, and so much more!

You are the God who speaks. Help me listen for Your voice. You are the God who rescues. Help me ask for Your saving. You are the God who loves. Give me the faith to accept Your love.

What's your favorite time of year? Are there things about your favorite season, holiday, or event that are only possible because of God—things that are impossible for humans to create or accomplish? Make a list of those "only God" things. (Remember, they exist because God spoke!)

....

....

....

....

....

....

....

....

....

....

....

....

....

....

Think about a season of the year and the beauty you see outside at that time. Draw a picture of things God created for us to enjoy in that season.

DRAW IT!

DO IT!

Go outside. Spend some time appreciating everything God spoke into existence. Then, because words are so important, say a prayer to God. Thank Him for everything He created for you to enjoy.

What did you learn from Hebrews 11:1–3 and 2 Corinthians 5:7?

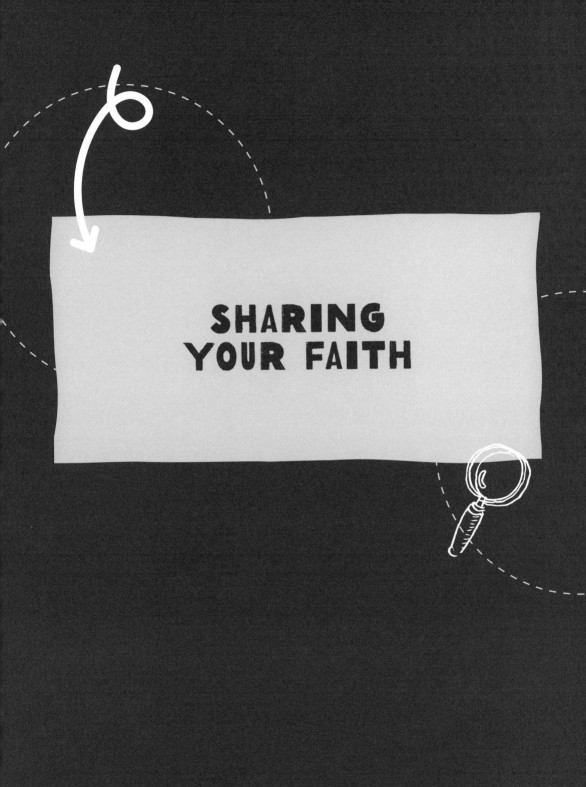

SHARING YOUR FAITH

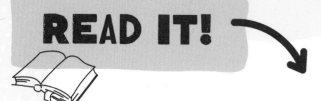

Your heart should be holy and set apart for the Lord God. Always be ready to tell everyone who asks you why you believe as you do. Be gentle as you speak and show respect.
1 PETER 3:15

If someone needs rescuing, they may not want to hear all the reasons why they need to be rescued. They just need help! When a house is on fire, the firefighters who show up don't stand outside with a megaphone, trying to convince the people inside that they need rescuing, do they?

There are ways to talk to people about their need for Jesus—none of which involve shrieking at the top of our lungs that they need His rescue. Romans 1:16 says, "I am not ashamed of the Good News. It is the power of God. It is the way He saves." We should always be ready to share God with anyone willing to listen. But we should always share Him with gentleness and respect.

Your Word helps me know You better, Lord. Your Word helps me know how to share You with others. Give me the right words. Remind me to be gentle and respectful at all times. I want to speak helpful words about You, my good, caring, loving, and kind Father.

....

....

....

....

....

....

....

....

....

....

....

....

....

....

WRITE IT!

Do you have a "rescue story" about the time when someone
shared God with you and you said yes to His invitation?
If your life was changed because someone shared their
faith with you, write a letter to that special person.
Thank him or her for introducing you to God. Then drop
your letter in the mail or hand-deliver it if you can.

....

....

....

....

....

....

....

....

....

....

....

....

....

Draw a picture of what it looks like to share God with someone else. (What would you be doing? What would the other person be doing?)

DRAW IT!

DO IT!

If you've never shared your faith with someone else, practice with your mom or dad—or a good friend. Ask God to give you the right words. Ask God to open the hearts of those who don't know Him. Then, even if it's hard, take the next step and share God with someone who needs His rescue.

What did you learn from 1 Peter 3:15 and Romans 1:16?

....

....

....

....

....

....

....

....

....

....

....

....

....

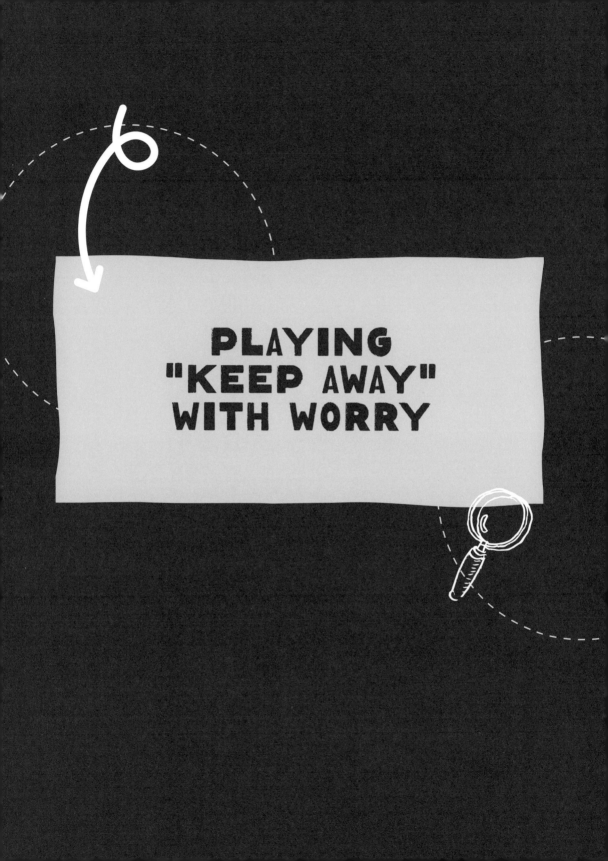

PLAYING
"KEEP AWAY"
WITH WORRY

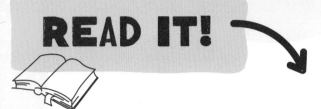

Do not worry. Learn to pray about everything. Give thanks to God as you ask Him for what you need. The peace of God is much greater than the human mind can understand. This peace will keep your hearts and minds through Christ Jesus.

PHILIPPIANS 4:6–7

If you really trust someone who makes a promise to you, you don't worry. You believe that if they say they'll do something, then they'll do it. It might not be easy to *never* worry, but when you're worry-free, you're grateful and filled with peace. Isaiah 26:3 says, "You will keep the man in perfect peace whose mind is kept on You, because he trusts in You."

When you worry, it might be because you're not fully trusting that God will take care of you. Try to keep worry away by trusting that God is who He says He is and that He will do what He promised. It's amazing how you change for the better when you leave God in charge of your life!

I want to believe that You know and want what's best for me, Father. I don't want to worry. Help me trust that You can—and will!—always do what I can't. And because You love me, You will give me just the help I need when I need it.

PRAY IT!

....

....

....

....

....

....

....

....

....

....

....

....

....

....

....

WRITE IT!

Finish these prayers.

God, when I worry I...

....
....
....
....
....

God, when I trust You I...

....
....
....
....
....

God, I am most at peace when...

....
....
....
....

Draw a picture of something that causes you to worry. When you're finished, say a prayer asking God to give you peace.

DRAW IT!

DO IT!

Make a "worry jar." Every time you worry, write it down on a slip of paper, pray about it, and then place it in your worry jar as a sign that you're letting God take care of it!

What did you learn from Philippians 4:6–7 and Isaiah 26:3?

FORGIVING AND BEING FORGIVEN

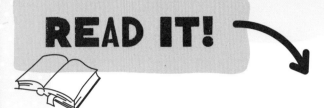

[God] has not paid us back for all our wrong-doings. For His loving-kindness for those who fear Him is as great as the heavens are high above the earth. He has taken our sins from us as far as the east is from the west. The Lord has loving-pity on those who fear Him, as a father has loving-pity on his children. For He knows what we are made of. He remembers that we are dust.
PSALM 103:10–14

When you break God's rules, you need to be forgiven. If He couldn't forgive you, then you could never be close to God. And your close relationship is very important to Him—that's why He made a way to forgive you. First John 1:9 says, "If we tell Him our sins, He is faithful and we can depend on Him to forgive us of our sins. He will make our lives clean from all sin." When you need forgiveness, go to Him in prayer and ask Him for it.

God will forgive you, but He asks you to follow His example and forgive those who have hurt you too. Don't seek revenge; offer forgiveness instead.

It's usually easier to be angry with people than to forgive them, God. Forgiveness is hard! Please help me understand why forgiveness is so important to You. I want forgiveness to be that important to me too.

WRITE IT!

Make a list of all the reasons why it's hard to forgive someone who has hurt you. Then write these words beneath: "I hurt God, and yet He forgave me." Then spend time thinking about which words on the page are more important: your list of reasons or God's gift of forgiveness.

Draw a picture of what a happy, forgiven face looks like.

DRAW IT!

DO IT!

Is there someone who needs your forgiveness today? Once you've thought about it, give that person a call, send a text, or write a letter letting them know that you care about them, that God cares about them, and that they're forgiven!

What did you learn from Psalm 103:10–14 and 1 John 1:9?

RECEIVING AND SHARING KINDNESS

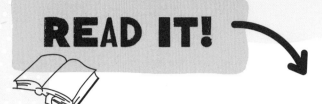

READ IT!

> *"Love those who hate you. Do good to them. Let them use your things and do not expect something back. Your reward will be much. You will be the children of the Most High. He is kind to those who are not thankful and to those who are full of sin."*
> LUKE 6:35

Kindness has nothing to do with what's fair. In fact, kindness is doing good things for other people even when they don't deserve it. Think about it: God has *always* done this for you—He has always been kind. Romans 2:4 says, "Do you forget about His loving-kindness to you? Do you forget how long He is waiting for you? You know that God is kind."

Forgiveness is kind. Love is kind. God is love, and He is kind. He wants you to understand the value of kindness in your life and in the lives of others. Kindness is super important and has the potential to change the world! God's kindness is worth receiving and sharing.

Your kindness is what encourages me to be close to You, Father. If You weren't kind, it would be hard to trust You. Thanks for showing me that kindness is possible no matter what, and it's how You want us to share Your love with others.

....

....

....

....

....

....

....

....

....

....

....

....

....

WRITE IT!

Write about a time when someone showed you kindness. How did it make you feel? How was it different than when someone was unkind? Why do you think God wants kindness to be your response?

Kindness is God's idea.
Draw a picture of you showing
kindness to someone else.

DRAW IT!

DO IT!

It's experiment time! Be kind to someone you know (a friend or family member) and then be kind to someone you don't know very well (not a stranger). Is it easier to be kind to the people you know or the people you don't?

What did you learn from Luke 6:35 and Romans 2:4?

....

....

....

....

....

....

....

....

....

....

....

....

....

HELPING, GIVING, SHARING

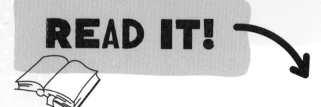

God has given each of you a gift. Use it to help each other. This will show God's loving-favor. . . . If a man helps others, let him do it with the strength God gives. So in all things God may be honored through Jesus Christ.
1 PETER 4:10–11

It's not natural for people to help each other, so God has shown us how it's done. It's not natural to be kind to others, but it's how God shows us who He is. It's not natural to share with others, but when you had nothing, God gave you exactly what you needed. These things—helping, being kind, and sharing—mean a lot to God, and He wants them to mean a lot to you too. Proverbs 11:25 says, "The man who gives much will have much, and he who helps others will be helped himself."

You will never lose when you do what God asks you to do. You can give because He gave to you, and you can keep on sharing because He'll always keep on sharing with you.

Keeping what I have makes sense to me, Lord. You give, and it makes sense to You. Help me remember that You *never* run out of what I need. So when I share—even if it's a lot!—I'll still always have the good gifts You give.

WRITE IT!

Write about a giving experience. It could
be something you gave, something you received,
or something you saw someone else give or receive.
Why is this experience something you remember?

Draw three things that you really love but would be willing to share.

DRAW IT!

DO IT!

Create a coupon for someone in your family. The coupon should be redeemable for time together spent doing something that person will enjoy. Offer to help complete a chore even when no one has asked you to. How did these acts of kindness make you feel?

What did you learn from 1 Peter 4:10–11 and Proverbs 11:25?

....

....

....

....

....

....

....

....

....

....

....

....

DOING THINGS
GOD'S WAY

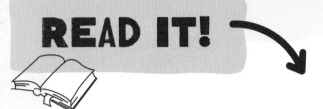
*"Be strong and have strength of heart!
Do not be afraid or lose faith. For the Lord
your God is with you anywhere you go."*
JOSHUA 1:9

The way God wants things done is very different from the way people do things. People are selfish; God shares. People refuse to forgive; forgiving is God's first response. People hate; God loves. Doing things God's way may seem hard. But Galatians 6:9 says, "Do not let yourselves get tired of doing good. If we do not give up, we will get what is coming to us at the right time."

If you want to do things God's way, you'll need lots of courage. Some people think it's pointless to help others. But you know that it's important to help because that's what God wants you to do. And you're following God, not other people. If others don't understand why you do things differently than most, introduce them to the one who has a good reason for doing things differently—God!

I want to be a courageous young man, God. Please help me become strong enough to do what You ask and humble enough to know I need Your help. I want to live Your way, Father.

....

....

....

....

....

....

....

....

....

....

....

....

....

....

Write about something God wants you to do that requires courage. Is what He's asking you to do difficult? Why do you think it's important to do what God asks, even when you're afraid or maybe just don't feel like it?

....

....

....

....

....

....

....

....

....

....

....

....

....

....

....

Draw a picture of yourself
being brave for God.

DRAW IT!

God can help you when you can't help yourself. He also helps when you ask. And asking for help takes courage. It also takes courage to do the right thing. Make a list of five "right things" you can do today. Then go out and do them! Place an X beside every item you accomplish. (Did you remember to ask God for help?)

What did you learn from Joshua 1:9 and Galatians 6:9?

UNDERSTANDING WHAT GOD WANTS YOU TO DO

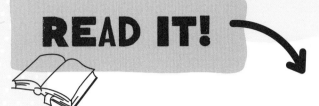

> *Be careful how you live. Live as men who are wise and not foolish. Make the best use of your time. These are sinful days. Do not be foolish. Understand what the Lord wants you to do.*
> EPHESIANS 5:15–17

God wants you to walk with Him, but He wants you to know *why* you walk with Him and *where* your walk with Him will take you. He wants you to obey His rules, and He provides all the details in His Word so you can do just that. James 1:5 says, "If you do not have wisdom, ask God for it. He is always ready to give it to you and will never say you are wrong for asking."

Your walk with God is not a guessing game. He doesn't hide truth from you. His Word has details about living your best life with Him in the lead. If God asks you to do something, it's for your good! Every rule or requirement He has is for His good purpose!

I don't want to be foolish, Father. I want to read the Bible to know more about You and Your rules for my life. And when I pray, I need Your help remembering what I read and then doing what You ask.

....

....

....

....

....

....

....

....

....

....

....

....

....

....

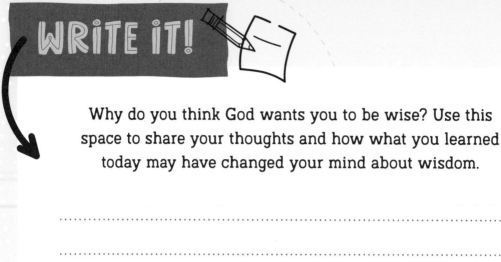

WRITE IT!

Why do you think God wants you to be wise? Use this space to share your thoughts and how what you learned today may have changed your mind about wisdom.

....

....

....

....

....

....

....

....

....

....

....

....

....

Draw a picture of yourself doing something that shows you using God's wisdom for your life.

DRAW IT!

DO IT!

Can you do a lot of things better today than you did when you were six years old? Of course! With practice, you can improve at nearly everything! Thank God for giving you wisdom and for helping you learn how to do new things and to do old things even better. Invite your mom or dad into a conversation about wisdom and how you've improved at things as you've grown through the years.

What did you learn from Ephesians 5:15–17 and James 1:5?

....

....

....

....

....

....

....

....

....

....

....

....

....

DEVELOPING CHARACTER

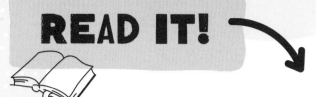

READ IT!

Troubles help us learn not to give up. When we have learned not to give up, it shows we have stood the test. When we have stood the test, it gives us hope. Hope never makes us ashamed because the love of God has come into our hearts through the Holy Spirit Who was given to us.
ROMANS 5:3–5

What is character? If you're not sure, character is who you really are as a person. It's what you do and the choices you make when no one is looking. Your character becomes stronger as time passes. The Bible talks a lot about character. Romans 12:2 says, "Do not act like the sinful people of the world. Let God change your life. First of all, let Him give you a new mind. Then you will know what God wants you to do. And the things you do will be good and pleasing and perfect."

The change God can bring to your life is what helps you develop the new, improved character He wants for you!

Help me move closer to the more improved version of me that You want me to be, Father. Grow my character so the things I do and decisions I make when I'm by myself match the choices and decisions I make when I'm around other people. I want my character to please You.

WRITE IT!

What does Godlike character look like? Make a
list of things you could do to grow your character.
Then describe how you plan to make that happen.

....

....

....

....

....

....

....

....

....

....

....

....

....

....

....

Draw a picture of someone you know who has great character. This is a picture of _____.

DRAW IT!

DO IT!

The longer you're friends with God, the greater influence He has over your choices. A choice can become a habit—and that makes an impact, for good or for bad, on your character. Choose three character traits (examples include compassion, creativity, and obedience), and make a plan for how you will build those in your life this week—and in the weeks to come.

What did you learn from Romans 5:3–5 and Romans 12:2?

BEING A GOOD FRIEND

READ IT!

God has chosen you. You are holy and loved by Him. Because of this, your new life should be full of loving-pity. You should be kind to others and have no pride. Be gentle and be willing to wait for others. Try to understand other people. Forgive each other. If you have something against someone, forgive him. That is the way the Lord forgave you. And to all these things, you must add love. Love holds everything and everybody together and makes all these good things perfect.
COLOSSIANS 3:12–14

In His Word, God shows you how to be a good friend. You can start by being kind and gentle. Try to understand what others are going through in life. Forgive them when they disappoint you. God has been a wonderful friend to you, and so you should be this kind of friend to others. First Thessalonians 5:11 says, "Comfort each other and make each other strong." That's good advice between friends.

If you want to have great friends, then be a great friend. This is how God started His friendship with you. He didn't wait to be kind. He didn't wait to show compassion. He was kind and compassionate from the very start! He was a friend to you first!

God, thank You for being my friend even when I thought I didn't need You in my life. Thank You for helping me see for myself what real friendship looks like because You have been such a good friend to me. Thank You for Your friendship that has changed my life.

PRAY IT!

WRITE IT!

Finish these sentences.

I am a friend of God because...

....
....
....
....
....
....

I can be a friend to others because...

....
....
....
....
....
....

Draw a picture of your best friend.

DRAW IT!

Sit down with your best friend and have a conversation about friendship. Discuss how you both might do better—at being kind, gentle, patient, understanding, forgiving, and loving.

What did you learn from Colossians 3:12–14 and 1 Thessalonians 5:11?

....

....

....

....

....

....

....

....

....

....

....

....

....

MEETING THE NEEDS OF FAMILY

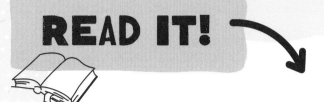

"I will be a Father to you. You will be My sons and daughters, says the All-powerful God."
2 Corinthians 6:18

You have a family—including your parents, siblings, grandparents, aunts and uncles and cousins—but when you said yes to Jesus, you also became part of His family. Your relatives can help take care of your physical—and even some of your emotional—needs. But God, who is your heavenly Father, takes care of *everything*! Each of your needs is known to God, and He can take care of every single one. Romans 8:15 says, "The Holy Spirit makes us [God's] sons, and we can call to Him, 'My Father.' "

God's idea for family is that each person works together to meet needs. When they can't meet a need (or won't), then God will take care of it. This is also why other Christians are so important. They are part of God's family—and they can become the family you need too! God knows that human families aren't perfect, and so His plan for making you part of His bigger Christian family was a very good idea, don't you think?

Thank You for each person in my family, Lord. I love and appreciate every single one of them! I am also thankful that You're my heavenly Father. I'm so glad that when You called me, I said yes and became Your son! Thanks for being my friend and for showing me the best a family has to offer.

PRAY IT!

WRITE IT!

Make a list of all the good things you love about your family, and then write down all the good things about being part of God's family. (Be sure to say thanks to God for both!)

....

....

....

....

....

....

....

....

....

....

....

....

....

....

Draw a picture of your favorite family memory.

DRAW IT!

DO IT!

Are there some wonderful things about God's family that you don't recognize in your family at home? Don't get upset. Instead, ask God to help you be a good example to your family. Help your family the way God helps you. Start today!

What did you learn from 2 Corinthians 6:18 and Romans 8:15?

....

....

....

....

....

....

....

....

....

....

....

....

....

HAVING AN OBEDIENT HEART

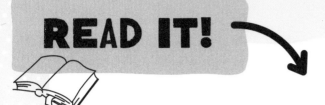

READ IT!

[Jesus said,] "The one who loves Me is the one who has My teaching and obeys it. My Father will love whoever loves Me. I will love him and will show Myself to him."
JOHN 14:21

God asks you to obey. Obeying means that you're willing to do what God tells you to do. One of the best reasons to obey God is because all of His requests and commands are good. He won't ever ask you to do anything that would harm you or others. First Peter 1:14 says, "Be like children who obey. Do not desire to sin like you used to when you did not know any better."

When you do what God says, you show that you trust His love—even though you may not fully understand Him. But the more you obey God, the better you'll begin to understand who He is and why He demands certain things of you. Ask God to help you remember that His commands are part of the way He loves you and cares for you. And He loves and cares for you more than anyone else on the planet!

Where You want me to walk, turn my feet in that direction, Lord. Whatever You tell me to avoid, it's because You love me and want only the best for me. And so I need to obey. Help me to trust You enough to always do what You ask.

WRITE IT!

Finish these sentences.

Today I will obey God by. . .

....

....

....

....

....

....

....

It's important for me to obey Him because. . .

....

....

....

....

....

....

....

Draw a picture that shows you being obedient to God.

DO IT!

Don't wait to be asked to do something. When you see your mom or dad doing a household chore, ask how you can help—and then do it! Make it a goal to be obedient to God—and to Mom and Dad—every single day. Read God's Word and do what it says.

What did you learn from John 14:21 and 1 Peter 1:14?

....

....

....

....

....

....

....

....

....

....

....

....

....

....

LOVING OTHERS

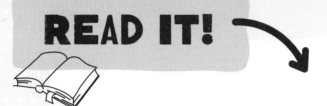

READ IT!

[Jesus said,] "I give you a new Law. You are to love each other. You must love each other as I have loved you. If you love each other, all men will know you are My followers."
JOHN 13:34–35

Loving God probably seems easy because He's perfect and always keeps His promises. Loving human beings is a different story—they aren't so easy to love. People aren't perfect, and they often break their promises. But God wants you to practice loving others as you're learning from His Word. Ephesians 4:2 says, "Be gentle and kind. Do not be hard on others. Let love keep you from doing that."

This verse from Ephesians isn't just a suggestion for how you should treat other people. It's God's law (a command), and it is meant to be followed. God gave you a great reason to love others, and it's this: He loved you first. When you love God and then love everyone else, it helps other people to recognize that you made the choice to follow God. When you show love, it makes you stand out—because showing love isn't what every person does. Maybe that's why God wants you to make loving others a priority—and so, you should!

Help me to always choose love over hate, Father—even when it's the hard choice. Remind me that what You ask me to do is what You *already* do. When You ask me to love You, I need to remember that You can help me to love others well too. You can make the impossible possible.

WRITE IT!

What are five ways you can show love to others?

1. ....
   ....
2. ....
   ....
3. ....
   ....
4. ....
   ....
5. ....
   ....

What are five ways you can show love to God?

1. ....
   ....
2. ....
   ....
3. ....
   ....
4. ....
   ....
5. ....
   ....

Draw a picture of how you feel when you are loved. (Imagine how someone else will feel if you show love to them.)

DRAW IT!

DO IT!

It's time to practice what you've learned about love. Find someone in your home who is willing to help you. Ask that person to pretend to be crabby or upset, and then you can practice what you've learned about kindness, compassion, and love.

What did you learn from John 13:34–35 and Ephesians 4:2?

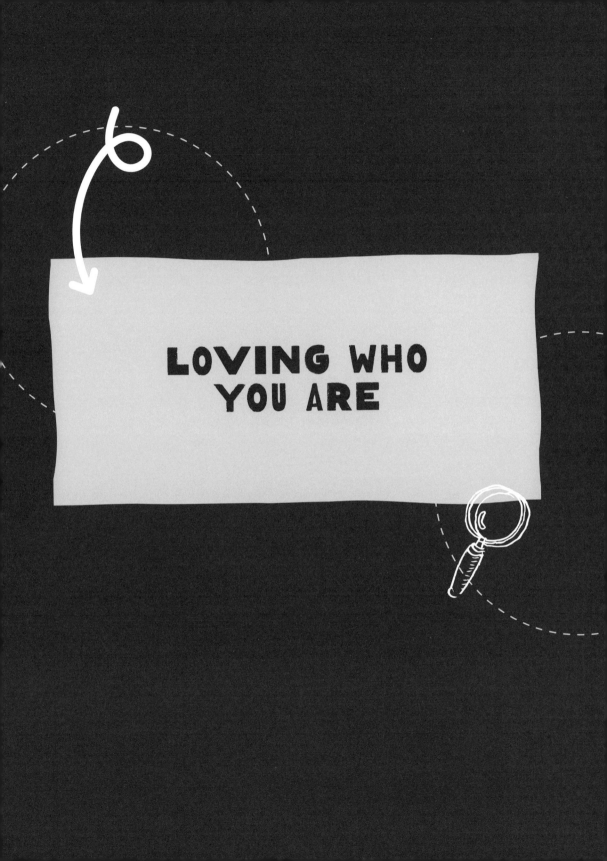

LOVING WHO
YOU ARE

You made the parts inside me. You put me together inside my mother. I will give thanks to You, for the greatness of the way I was made brings fear. Your works are great and my soul knows it very well. My bones were not hidden from You when I was made in secret and put together with care in the deep part of the earth.
PSALM 139:13–15

God made you. You're different from anyone else in the whole wide world. Even if you look a lot like someone else in your family (or maybe you're a twin), you still have your own thoughts and unique characteristics. Isn't that amazing? If you ever feel like you're not very special, remember that God not only made you, but He has a plan for your life. Ephesians 5:29 says, "No man hates himself. He takes care of his own body. That is the way Christ does. He cares for His body which is the church."

So, young man, take care of yourself. Love the person God made you to be. Obey what He says. When you trust and obey the God who made you, you make yourself available to Him by doing important things for His family—the kingdom of God!

Sometimes I don't like myself very much, God—but You always do! In fact, You *love* me! And You want me to remember that You made me, forgive me, and care for me. What You love is also what I should love—and so there's never any moment I should dislike me (or anyone else!).

WRITE IT!

List five things that make you unique.

1. ....

2. ....

3. ....

4. ....

5. ....

Now write a prayer thanking God for making you *you*!

....

....

....

....

....

....

....

....

....

....

....

Draw a picture of something unique about you.

DRAW IT!

DO IT!

Have a discussion with a trusted adult about all the special things they have noticed about you. Explain that you're trying to learn all the ways God made you unique. Be sure to say thank-you after your conversation, and say a big thank-you to God for the people who see the good in you—even when you can't always see it for yourself!

What did you learn from Psalm 139:13–15 and Ephesians 5:29?

PRAYING ALWAYS

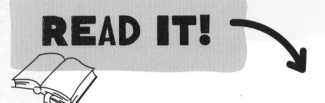

READ IT!

Do not worry. Learn to pray about everything. Give thanks to God as you ask Him for what you need. The peace of God is much greater than the human mind can understand. This peace will keep your hearts and minds through Christ Jesus.
PHILIPPIANS 4:6–7

There's a feeling that you've probably experienced—one that makes you unsettled. It makes you think *the worst thing ever* is going to happen. It makes it hard to sleep. This feeling is worry. You might not know that worry is a choice people make. People often choose to worry because they think they might change how things turn out just by worrying a little bit more. But the truth is they can't change one single thing by worrying. God said in Jeremiah 33:3, "Call to Me, and I will answer you. And I will show you great and wonderful things which you do not know."

When you're worried, the best thing you can do is to pray—every chance you get. When you pray, it shows God that you believe He can handle anything. In prayer, you share your greatest fears, biggest dreams, and most urgent concerns. Prayer should never be the last thing you do—it should always come first! God has all the answers to every one of your worries.

It's never a bad time to talk to You, Lord. You want me to talk to You every moment of the day. And You want me to stop worrying about things You can easily take care of. Give me peace. Help me sleep. When I'm worried, remind me to talk to You first.

PRAY IT!

WRITE IT!

Share about a time when you were
worried and how prayer helped.

....

....

....

....

....

....

....

....

....

....

....

....

....

....

....

Draw a picture of you praying
in your favorite place.

DRAW IT!

DO IT!

Put prayer into practice! Every time a worry creeps into your mind, send up a prayer to God. Tell Him that you're giving your worry to Him and that you trust He has it under control. Do this for a few weeks and see how you grow in your faith. Once you've experienced how prayer makes a huge difference in your life, share what you've learned with someone you know who worries a lot.

What did you learn from Philippians 4:6–7 and Jeremiah 33:3?

DISCOVERING GOD'S PLANS

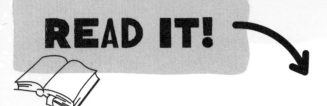

Listen! You who say, "Today or tomorrow we will go to this city and stay a year and make money." You do not know about tomorrow. What is your life? It is like fog. You see it and soon it is gone. What you should say is, "If the Lord wants us to, we will live and do this or that."
JAMES 4:13–15

What do you want to be when you grow up? You might have an idea, but you shouldn't be surprised if it changes (sometimes more than once!). The best thing you can do is ask God to help guide you to what you should do in the future. Jeremiah 29:11 says, " 'I know the plans I have for you,' says the Lord, 'plans for well-being and not for trouble, to give you a future and a hope.' "

If you insist on making every decision about your future, then you may be dissatisfied with the result, or you might just miss out on the very thing that gives your life purpose. So, young man, invite God into your plans and allow Him to point you in the best direction.

I don't want to get ahead of You, Father. Because You have good plans for me, I only want to run toward the future You've set in motion for me. I don't ever want to choose what's second best. Give me a heart that recognizes and obeys Your direction and a mind that's willing to learn from You.

....

....

....

....

....

....

....

....

....

....

....

....

....

....

Is there anything that makes you question God's plans for your future? Are you afraid He might ask you to do something you don't want to do? Write about it in the space below.

....

....

....

....

....

....

....

....

....

....

....

....

....

....

....

....

Draw a picture of the future you.

DRAW IT!

DO IT!

Ask a trusted adult who loves Jesus to share their story with you. Ask how God helped them know the direction they should take. Find out if they ever questioned God's plan and how they handled any doubt. Ask for their number one piece of advice for trusting God with the future—then write it down and hang it up somewhere you can see it every day!

What did you learn from James 4:13–15 and Jeremiah 29:11?

SURVIVING DIFFICULT TIMES

We are glad for our troubles also. We know that troubles help us learn not to give up. When we have learned not to give up, it shows we have stood the test. When we have stood the test, it gives us hope. Hope never makes us ashamed because the love of God has come into our hearts through the Holy Spirit Who was given to us.
ROMANS 5:3–5

Wanting what you want when you want it is normal. However, it's probably not what God wants for you. When you always get what you want, it doesn't teach you how to deal with hard things. And difficult times show up when you least expect them. Those moments look very different as you grow up. Hard things when you're three years old are quite different from hard things when you're twenty-five. James 1:2–4 says, "You should be happy when you have all kinds of tests. You know these prove your faith. It helps you not to give up. Learn well how to wait."

No one wants to experience hard things. The bad news? Hard things will come. But there's also some very good news: God can help you survive all of it! In hard times, you can have courage, strength, hope, and even joy—all because of God's love.

I can't run away from hard things, God—but boy, I sure wish I could. When I struggle, help me run to You first. Help me trust You enough to hold on through each difficult moment and feel Your love, strength, hope, and joy.

PRAY IT!

WRITE IT!

Share your thoughts by completing the following sentences:

When I face difficult moments, I usually. . .

....

....

....

....

....

....

....

With God in my life, I can live through
difficult moments because. . .

....

....

....

....

....

....

....

Draw a picture of you running God's race. What are you running toward?

DRAW IT!

On a poster board or large piece of construction paper, design and color a sign that says WHEN HARD TIMES COME, I WILL RUN TO GOD. Hang it up in your room where you'll see it every day.

What did you learn from Romans 5:3–5 and James 1:2–4?

....

....

....

....

....

....

....

....

....

....

....

....

....

UNDERSTANDING EMOTIONS

READ IT!

The fruit that comes from having the Holy Spirit in our lives is: love, joy, peace, not giving up, being kind, being good, having faith, being gentle, and being the boss over our own desires. The Law is not against these things.
GALATIANS 5:22–23

The "fruit" God wants to grow in your life will control your emotions. For instance, love is an emotion—but it's also a choice. Kindness can make someone feel good—but it also starts with a choice. God doesn't discourage emotions altogether. Every human being experiences a variety of emotions. But the important thing to understand is that emotions are unreliable because they sometimes don't tell the truth, and they sometimes lead you to do the wrong thing.

For example, you might be really, *really* mad, and your emotions tell you to throw a fit and yell at someone. If you allow your emotions to control you when you're super mad, you'll probably do something you regret. One of the fruits of the Spirit is self-control, or being boss over our desires. We can and must allow the Holy Spirit to control our emotions. Ecclesiastes 3:4 says, "There is a time to cry, and a time to laugh; a time to have sorrow, and a time to dance."

The tricky part about emotions is learning how to know when they are misleading you. You can learn to push emotions aside and make decisions based on the truth of God's Word—even when you don't "feel" like it. It's a big part of growing up.

I want to be wise enough to recognize when my emotions are telling me something different from what I should *really* be feeling and doing, Father. Help me remember that Your truth is *still* the truth, even when I don't feel like I want to believe it.

WRITE IT!

Write down some of the emotions you experienced today. Place them in a column on the left. Then think about how those emotions might lie to you—write about it next to each emotion you have listed.

How can you tell when your emotions are misleading you?

....

....

....

....

....

....

....

....

....

....

....

....

....

Imagine you experience the emotion of anger, but the truth says you should love and forgive instead. Draw a picture showing a time your anger turned to love.

DRAW IT!

Take the emotion list you created on page 130. Stand in front of a mirror and make the face you might make if you were to experience that emotion. Do you like what you see? How can God's truth change the way you look?

What did you learn from Galatians 5:22–23 and Ecclesiastes 3:4?

....

....

....

....

....

....

....

....

....

....

....

....

TRUSTING THAT GOD IS BIGGER THAN YOUR FEAR

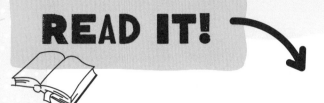

When I am afraid, I will trust in You. I praise the Word of God. I have put my trust in God. I will not be afraid. What can only a man do to me?
PSALM 56:3–4

Fear is an emotion that usually shows up when you think something bad is going to happen. Your brain tells you to be afraid because this terrible thing *will* happen, you just know it. The problem with this is that we are (or become) afraid of a lot of things that will *never* happen to us. Fear is one of the emotions that lies to and misleads us—*a lot!* Second Timothy 1:7 says, "God did not give us a spirit of fear. He gave us a spirit of power and of love and of a good mind."

Spend some time thinking about what God wants for you. The best thing to remember is that God has promised to take care of you. For those who have invited Jesus into their hearts, He has promised a forever home in heaven with Him. He has promised never-ending love and forgiveness. But fear will step in and try to convince you that none of God's promises are true. When you have a choice between the things fear tells you and what God promises, there's one clear choice every single time!

I don't want to listen to fear, God. I'm only interested in what You have to say. Help me to read, believe, and understand Your promises. I choose to trust You so fear won't make a home in my mind and heart.

PRAY IT!

What are you afraid of? Make a list below.
When you've completed your list, write,
"God is bigger than. . ." at the top of the page.
Then reread your list, starting with
the words you just added.

....

....

....

....

....

....

....

....

....

....

....

....

....

Draw a picture of something
that makes you feel brave.

DRAW IT!

DO IT!

Make a card that says "Trust God." Keep it in your pocket. And when you are afraid, grab it and read it out loud. Then say a prayer to God, thanking Him for giving you courage and strength.

What did you learn from Psalm 56:3–4 and 2 Timothy 1:7?

....
....
....
....
....
....
....
....
....
....
....
....
....
....

USING GOD'S GOOD GIFTS

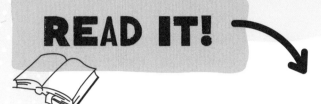

There are different kinds of gifts. But it is the same Holy Spirit Who gives them. There are different kinds of work to be done for Him. But the work is for the same Lord. There are different ways of doing His work. But it is the same God who uses all these ways in all people.
1 Corinthians 12:4–6

God offers you lots of gifts—and they're all very good. He starts with love and forgiveness and keeps on giving! You can experience His gifts of peace and courage too. What's super cool about God's gifts is that you can share them with others. First Peter 4:10 says, "God has given each of you a gift. Use it to help each other. This will show God's loving-favor."

When you're generous, it helps others see the value in the gifts God gives. Some people will only begin to discover God because of your willingness to share your gifts with them—especially when you give without asking for or expecting anything in return. That's true, unselfish giving! When you use God's gifts to help others, you are doing God's kingdom work. And God will bless you with more good gifts!

Thanks for giving me such good gifts, Father. Help me to be wise enough to accept what You offer. Help me to be kind enough to share what You give. Help me to be courageous enough to tell others where to find these really good gifts for themselves.

WRITE IT!

What is your favorite gift that God has given you?
Write it in the space below and explain why it's your favorite.
Then list five ways you can share this gift with others.

....

....

....

....

....

....

....

....

....

....

....

....

....

Draw a picture of you being generous and sharing one of God's gifts with a friend or family member.

DRAW IT!

DO IT!

You wrote it down, and now it's time to put your thoughts into action! Take your list from page 142, and then make a plan to share your gift with others this week. Share your plan with a parent or other trusted adult who can follow up with you and discuss what you learned from living out your faith.

What did you learn from 1 Corinthians 12:4–6 and 1 Peter 4:10?

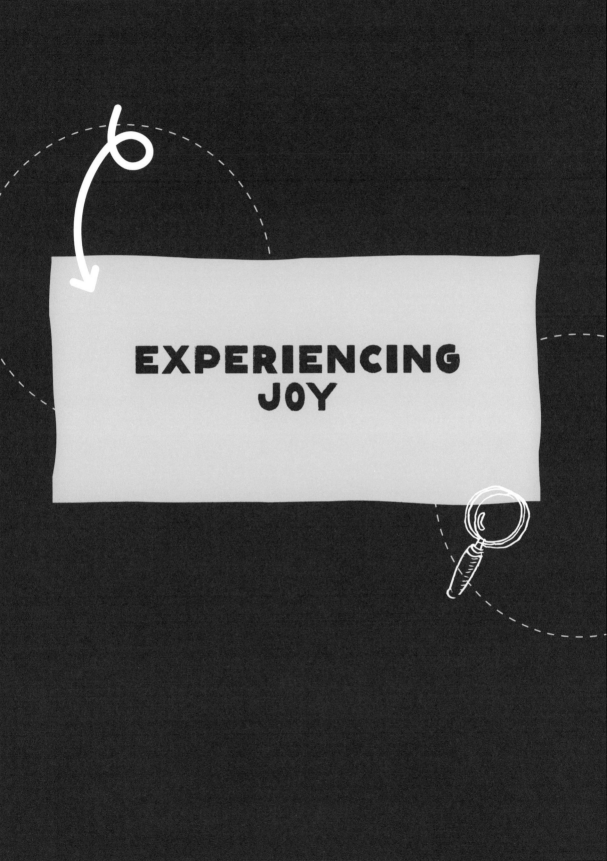

EXPERIENCING JOY

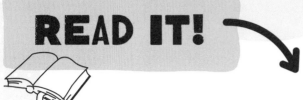

Praise the Lord! Praise Him, O you who serve the Lord. Praise the name of the Lord. Let the name of the Lord be honored, now and forever. The name of the Lord is to be praised from the time the sun rises to when it sets. The Lord is high above all nations. His shining-greatness is above the heavens.
Psalm 113:1–4

Do you know what it means to rejoice? Rejoicing is when joy comes to the surface of your thoughts—it's when joy keeps coming so much that it overflows in your mind, heart, and spirit. And you think only of God and how good He is to you. Joy is so much more—*and better*—than happiness. Joy is knowing that God can make good things out of bad things. Joy is believing God can be trusted. Joy is constant, but happiness comes and goes. Philippians 4:4 says, "Be full of joy always because you belong to the Lord. Again I say, be full of joy!"

Today, rejoice in this: you're not an outsider or a misfit—not in God's eyes! He wants to be close to you; He wants to walk with you; He wants to help you. Let the joy you experience spill over to others. Help them see that your trust in God is moving your life in a very good direction.

I want my words and actions to show You just how thankful I am, Lord. Let joy keep changing me for good. May joy keep my words focused on praising You. I want to rediscover joy in You every day of my life!

Think of a time when you
experienced true joy. How did it change your
day? Why do you think it's important to God that
you find joy even when things are hard?

....

....

....

....

....

....

....

....

....

....

....

....

....

....

Draw a picture of something that brings you joy.

DRAW IT!

DO IT!

Make a list of things that bring you joy. Beside each, describe how God is a part of that joy you feel. Hang it on the refrigerator and invite your family members to add to the list!

What did you learn from Psalm 113:1–4 and Philippians 4:4?

....

....

....

....

....

....

....

....

....

....

....

....

....

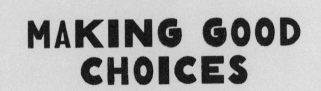

MAKING GOOD CHOICES

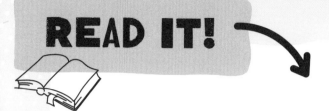
*Do you think I am trying to get the favor of men,
or of God? If I were still trying to please men,
I would not be a servant owned by Christ.*
GALATIANS 1:10

Everyone has an opinion about things. And it's important to know that sometimes opinions are wrong. A friend might suggest that you do something, and he believes it's not wrong to do it. He might suggest cheating or lying as an easy way to get out of a situation. But if you know God's Word, He says that cheating and lying will *never* be His plan for you. Proverbs 4:14–15 says, "Do not go on the path of the sinful. Do not walk in the way of bad men. Stay away from it. Do not pass by it. Turn from it, and pass on."

God doesn't want you to hate someone for suggesting a bad choice, but He does ask you to say no to the pressure you might feel to go along with the bad choice. When you have a choice to make, you can either fear the opinion of a friend or respect God and keep walking with Him. What will you choose?

I want to make good choices, Lord. I have friends who tell me that it's not so bad to do something You say is off-limits. Help me listen to You instead. Help me to be an example to my friends so I can teach them more about You and Your Word.

PRAY IT!

WRITE IT!

Who has your full attention? God or a friend? Why? When you have a choice to make, what—or who—can help you make the right one? Write your thoughts on the lines below.

....

....

....

....

....

....

....

....

....

....

....

....

....

....

Draw a picture of you making a choice and doing the right thing.

DRAW IT!

Create a "Bad Choice" versus "God's Best" game. Everyone who plays gets two cards: one with the words "Bad Choice" and one that says "God's Best." Each person takes turns creating scenarios in which a choice is made. Players then hold up the card that best matches the choice. Discussion about the best choice follows every turn. See if you or your friends can back up "God's Best" choices with scripture.

What did you learn from Galatians 1:10 and Proverbs 4:14–15?

STAYING
HUMBLE

God has given me His loving-favor.
This helps me write these things to you. I ask
each one of you not to think more of himself than
he should think. Instead, think in the right way
toward yourself by the faith God has given you.
ROMANS 12:3

Boys play games and sports to prove who is the better player. Everyone wants to be a winner, don't they? You might love the competition and the bragging rights that come with a win. And while games are a good way to learn about sportsmanship and fair play, sometimes pride can get in the way—especially if you're on a winning team. God's Word has something to say about the struggle you might have with pride. Proverbs 11:2 says, "When pride comes, then comes shame, but wisdom is with those who have no pride."

This doesn't mean you shouldn't feel content or satisfied when you do a good job or win a game, but it's important to know that very few people are interested in hearing you talk about how great you are. When you make things all about you, then you don't notice the great things God allows other people to accomplish. When you're tempted to be prideful, remember this: God loves you just the way you are (win or lose!), so you have nothing to prove to Him—ever!

You're the greatest, God. I can't compare to You. *No one can compare to You.* Still, You choose to love me, and You tell me to love others too. It's hard to love others well when I continually compare myself with other people in an effort to make myself look better than them. Give me the wisdom to love others the way You want me to love them, Lord. I want to stop the comparisons.

PRAY IT!

WRITE IT!

Answer these questions in the spaces below.

Why is it so tempting to compare yourself to other people?

....

....

....

What can you do to turn your focus away from comparing?

....

....

....

When you compare yourself to others, does it always make you feel better? Or does it make you feel worse?

....

....

....

Why is it important to God that you recognize the accomplishments of others?

....

....

....

Draw a picture of you cheering on the opposing team.

DRAW IT!

DO IT!

Practice good sportsmanship this week.
When another team wins, tell them, "Great game,"
and compliment some of the guys on their skills.

What did you learn from Romans 12:3 and Proverbs 11:2?

REFUSING TO CHOOSE ANGER

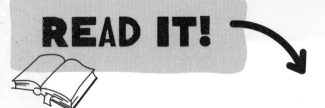

READ IT!

Stop being angry. Turn away from fighting.
Do not trouble yourself. It leads only to wrong-doing.
PSALM 37:8

People say hurtful things, and you get mad. People laugh at your mistakes, and you become bitter. People bully you, and you want to get even. One of the biggest problems with anger is that it makes you want to pay someone back for their bad choice, but seeking revenge only makes things worse. Proverbs 15:1 says, "A gentle answer turns away anger, but a sharp word causes anger."

You've heard sharp words that make you angry. You've also probably spoken sharp words that made someone else angry. Anger causes nations to go to war against each other. Anger destroys friendships. Anger makes it hard to think clearly. God says it's always better to use gentle words when you or someone else is upset. When you obey God, He can even use you to stop anger before it starts. With God's help, you can avoid anger, wrongdoing, and hurtful words and actions. Choose God—choose forgiveness and love.

Anger is like junk food, Lord. It tastes good while I'm "eating" anger—and I want more of it. But afterward it makes me sick to my stomach. Help me choose a response that can stop anger before it gets out of control. Help me avoid trouble by choosing love and forgiveness over anger.

PRAY IT!

WRITE IT!

Draw a line down the middle of the page. On the left side, list things that make you angry. On the right side, get creative about listing a response that stops anger in its tracks.

Things That
Make Me Angry

How I Can Stop
Anger in Its Tracks

Draw a picture of your angry face.
Then look in the mirror and smile.
Which face would people rather see?

DRAW IT!

DO IT!

Look back at page 166—paying special attention to what you wrote in the "How I Can Stop Anger in Its Tracks" column. When you find yourself getting angry this week, use some of your ideas to keep your anger under control, then say a prayer of thanks to God for His help.

What did you learn from Psalm 37:8 and Proverbs 15:1?

LIVING WITH GRATITUDE

Let the peace of Christ have power over your hearts. You were chosen as a part of His body. Always be thankful. Let the teaching of Christ and His words keep on living in you. These make your lives rich and full of wisdom. Keep on teaching and helping each other. Sing the Songs of David and the church songs and the songs of heaven with hearts full of thanks to God. Whatever you say or do, do it in the name of the Lord Jesus. Give thanks to God the Father through the Lord Jesus.

COLOSSIANS 3:15–17

When you're left out, instead of being angry, tell God thanks for welcoming you to His family. If someone says something mean, remember that God made you and that His kindness changed your life. Psalm 107:1 says, "Give thanks to the Lord for He is good! His loving-kindness lasts forever!"

When you embrace gratitude, it becomes easier to resist negative thoughts and emotions. What God has given you, no one can take away. God loves you more than anyone can hate. He forgives more than anyone can sin. With God in your life, there's so much to be thankful for! So, be a living thank-you note to God—a young man who lives each day with gratitude.

You're always kind and You love to bless, Father. Help me focus on Your goodness and always choose gratitude over anger and bitterness. Help me remember that when life doesn't turn out exactly the way I want it to, it's still the right story for my life because You wrote it and You are so, so good to me.

PRAY IT!

Finish this thought:

I am living a life of gratitude when I. . .

....

....

....

....

....

....

....

....

....

....

....

....

....

....

....

....

Draw a picture of something that makes you feel grateful.

DRAW IT!

DO IT!

Read Psalm 100. Use the words of this scripture passage to let God know you're grateful. Share what you're learning about gratitude with a family member or friend.

What did you learn from Colossians 3:15–17 and Psalm 107:1?

KNOWING
THE TRUTH

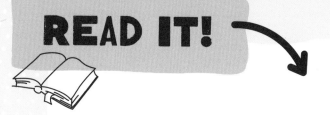

Jesus said, "I am the Way and the Truth and the Life. No one can go to the Father except by Me."
JOHN 14:6

You can ask a smart device in your home for information about something you want to know, but sometimes the information it gives you is wrong. You can ask a friend about something you need to know for class, but your friend might not have the right answer. You could ask a question, and someone who isn't a real friend might even lie to you. It's hard to know who to trust for reliable information. But there's good news—you can know the *truth*. John 17:17 says, "[God's] Word is truth."

Jesus said He is the Truth, and He also said that God's Word is truth. It just makes sense to look for truth from one reliable source, doesn't it? And God is that one reliable source! He never guesses, and He's not interested in confusing you. He doesn't change His mind about truth, and He doesn't pay attention to opinion polls.

Want a better handle on truth? Spend some time reading God's Word. Why? God *can't* lie—and He *won't*. He invites you on the path that leads directly to Him. His truth helps you get to know Him, and your life is made better when you trust Him as your friend and Savior. That's some awesome truth!

I never want to believe a lie, Lord, but at some point, I probably have. People sometimes say bad things about You and try to convince others that You aren't worth following. But if You are the Way, the Truth, and the Life, then I trust I won't find these things anywhere else. So, Lord, help me believe You and Your Word.

PRAY IT!

WRITE IT!

The Way. The Truth. The Life.
Think about what these words mean.
Jesus said He was all three.

How is Jesus the Way?

....
....
....
....

How is Jesus the Truth?

....
....
....
....

How is Jesus the Life?

....
....
....
....

Draw a picture of yourself reading
your Bible in your very favorite place.

DRAW IT!

DO IT!

God said that the Bible is good news and that His words are truth. Think about some ways to help your friends and family understand the importance of knowing God's truth and the importance of reading His Word. Start some conversations this week, and share what you've learned about truth.

What did you learn from John 14:6 and John 17:17?

LEARNING WHAT'S RIGHT

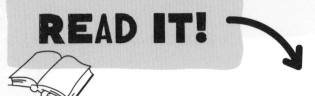

Happy is the man who does not walk in the way sinful men tell him to, or stand in the path of sinners, or sit with those who laugh at the truth. But he finds joy in the Law of the Lord and thinks about His Law day and night. This man is like a tree planted by rivers of water, which gives its fruit at the right time and its leaf never dries up. Whatever he does will work out well for him.

PSALM 1:1–3

You can do whatever you want (God gave you free will), but without knowing God's truth you're bound to make a bad decision. When you don't know the right thing to do, the best you can do is make a guess—but in the end, your decision might be harmful to yourself or someone else. Proverbs 12:15 says, "The way of a fool is right in his own eyes, but a wise man listens to good teaching."

When you learn what's right, you understand how God wants you to handle things. You learn to make decisions His way—which is always the very best way! If you don't know where to start, begin spending regular time in God's Word. Good decisions always include Him in the process. When you listen to His wisdom, you'll never go wrong.

Why would I ever want to make the wrong choice, God? I wouldn't! But I'm in danger of doing the wrong thing every time I forget to check in with You first. Help me remember to ask You before I make any decisions. I need Your help, Lord.

List five to ten things you should probably do or think about before making a big decision. Ask a parent or trusted adult to add a few more ideas to your list. Once it's complete, read over your list and spend some time considering why these things are so important.

....

....

....

....

....

....

....

....

....

....

....

....

Draw a picture of yourself
making a good decision.

DRAW IT!

DO IT!

Ask your family or a trusted friend to share about some choices they've made—both good and bad. Ask them for their advice as you grow into your teenage years and young adulthood. Make some notes you can look back on in the future when you're faced with hard decisions.

What did you learn from Psalm 1:1–3 and Proverbs 12:15?

FOLLOWING JESUS FOREVER

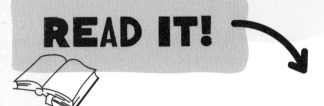
READ IT!

Jesus spoke to all the people, saying, "I am the Light of the world. Anyone who follows Me will not walk in darkness. He will have the Light of Life."
JOHN 8:12

You are nearing the end of this book, but if you know Jesus as your friend and Savior, your journey with Him will go on forever. Make sure you are following Him closely. Jesus' disciples had to make that choice, and so do you. In Matthew 16:24, Jesus said to His followers, "Follow Me."

When you walk with God, His light allows you to see where you should go. He provides the light to help make His teaching clear, His steps plain, and His way worth following. Will you say yes or no?

He will not make this choice for you. Instead, He invites you to follow Him and then waits for your decision. If you've already said yes, then keep walking, keep following, and keep making God your greatest pursuit. The journey you're on requires courage, but the best news is that God has chosen to walk with you—and whatever you need along the journey, He'll provide!

I sometimes struggle, Father. Not every day seems blessed. But when trouble comes, I'll do my best to remember that You walk with me. When I need comfort, You'll be there to tell me everything will work out for Your good.

PRAY IT!

WRITE IT!

If you have been following God, write about the
good things you have experienced so far because
He's in your life. Then write about what you look
forward to as you keep following Him.

....
....
....
....
....
....
....
....
....
....
....
....
....
....
....
....
....

Draw a picture of something you're looking forward to on your adventure with God.

DRAW IT!

DO IT!

Throughout the pages of this book, you've been challenged and encouraged to interact with trusted family and friends about what you're learning. Use this final activity to talk to those you love about the value of following God. Ask them to share their stories, and then share yours with them!

What did you learn from John 8:12 and Matthew 16:24?

....

....

....

....

....

....

....

....

....

....

....

....

....

....